D1025562

VOL. 6
Action Edition

Story and Art by
RUMIKO TAKAHASHI

English Adaptation by Gerard Jones

Translation/Mari Morimoto
Touch-Up Art & Lettering/Wayne Truman & Bill Schuch
Cover Design/Hidemi Sahara
Graphics & Design/Sean Lee
Editor (1st Edition)/Julie Davis
Editor (Action Edition)/Julie Davis

Managing Editor/Annette Roman
Editor in Chief/Alvin Lu
Sr. Dir. of Licensing and Acquisitions/Rika Inouye
VP of Sales & Marketing/Liza Coppola
Sr. VP of Editorial/Hyoe Narita
Publisher/Seiji Horibuchi

INUYASHA is rated "T+" for Older Teens. It may contain violence, language, alcohol or tobacco use, or suggestive situations.

Printed in Canada.

Published by VIZ, LLC
P.O. Box 77010
San Francisco, CA 94107

1st Edition published 2000

Action Edition
10 9 8 7 6 5 4 3
First printing, September 2003
Second printing, April 2004
Third printing, October 2004

VUYASH

VOL. 6

Action Editior

STORY AND ART BY

MIKO TAKAHAS

CONTENTS

Long ago, in the "Warring States" era of Japan's Muromachi period (Sengoku-jidai, approximately 1467-1568 CE), a legendary doglike half-demon called "Inu-Yasha" attempted to steal the Shikon Jewel, or "Jewel of Four Souls," from a village, but was stopped by the enchanted arrow of the village priestess, Kikyo. Inu-Yasha fell into a deep sleep, pinned to a tree by Kikyo's arrow, while the mortally wounded Kikyo took the Shikon Jewel with her into the fires of her funeral pyre. Years passed.

Fast forward to the present day. Kagome, a Japanese high school girl, is pulled into a well one day by a mysterious centipede monster, and finds herself transported into the past, only to come face to face with the trapped Inu-Yasha. She frees him, and Inu-Yasha easily defeats the centipede monster.

The residents of the village, now fifty years older, readily accept Kagome as the reincarnation of their deceased priestess Kikyo, a claim supported by the fact that the Shikon Jewel emerges from a cut on Kagome's body. Unfortunately, the jewel's rediscovery means that the village is soon under attack by a variety of demons in search of this treasure. Then, the jewel is accidentally shattered into many shards, each of which may have the fearsome power of the entire jewel.

Although Inu-Yasha says he hates Kagome because of her resemblance to Kikyo, the woman who "killed" him, he is forced to team up with her when Kaede, the village leader, binds him to Kagome with a powerful spell. Now the two grudging companions must fight to reclaim and reassemble the shattered shards of the Shikon Jewel before they fall into the wrong hands.

THIS VOLUME Kikyo is resurrected using Kagome's soul, and Inu-Yasha must choose whether to let her live or die.

CHARACTERS

INU-YASHA
A half-human, half-demon hybrid, Inu-Yasha has doglike ears, a thick mane of white hair, and demonic strength. Hoping to increase his demonic powers, he once stole the Shikon Jewel from a village, but was cast into a fifty-year sleep by the arrow of the village priestess, Kikyo, who died as a result of the battle. Now, he assists Kagome in her search for the shards of the Jewel, mostly because he has no choice in the matter—a charmed necklace allows Kagome to restrain him with a single word.

KAGOME
A Japanese schoolgirl from the modern day who is also the reincarnation of Kikyo, the priestess who imprisoned Inu-Yasha for fifty years with her enchanted arrow. As Kikyo's reincarnation, Kagome has the power to see the Shikon Jewel shards, even ones hidden within a demon's body.

KAEDE
Kikyo's little sister, who carried out the priestess' wish that the Shikon Jewel should be burned with her remains. Now fifty years older, Kaede is head of the village, and it is her spell that binds Inu-Yasha to Kagome by means of a string of prayer beads and Kagome's spoken word—"Sit!"

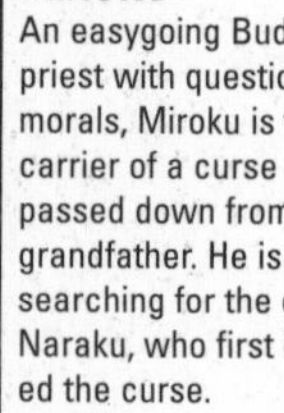

MIROKU
An easygoing Buddhist priest with questionable morals, Miroku is the carrier of a curse passed down from his grandfather. He is searching for the demon Naraku, who first inflicted the curse.

URASUE
A horrifying orgress with sorcerous powers, Urasue stole Kikyo's bones and resurrected the priestess by combining Kikyo's bones with Kagome's soul.

KIKYO
A powerful priestess, Kikyo was charged with the awesome responsibility of protecting the Shikon Jewel from demons and humans who coveted its power. She died after firing the enchanted arrow that kept Inu-Yasha imprisioned for fifty years.

MYOGA
Servant to Inu-Yasha, this flea-demon often offers sage advice, but he is also the first to flee when a situation turns dangerous. His bloodsucking seems to have the ability to weaken certain spells.

SHIPPO
A young fox-demon, orphaned by two other demons whose powers had been boosted by the Shikon Jewel, the mischievous Shippo enjoys goading Inu-Yasha and playing tricks with his shape-changing abilities.

SCROLL ONE

HATRED UNSPENT

KRII KRII
KIKYO...
THIS TIME I WON'T MISS.
SHHH...
YOU DO HATE ME, DON'T YOU?
FEH.

KIKYO... SISTER...
WILL YOU NOT REST UNTIL YOU HAVE SLAIN INU-YASHA ?
UNLESS HER SOUL TURNS AWAY FROM ITS OWN HATRED AND UNREST...
WHAT'S GONNA HAPPEN TO KAGOME ?
KAGOME...
KAGOME SHALL NEVER OPEN HER EYES AGAIN.
IT WILL NEVER RETURN TO THIS BODY.
SHUNNNG
HWOO
UHH !
SHHH
FWAA

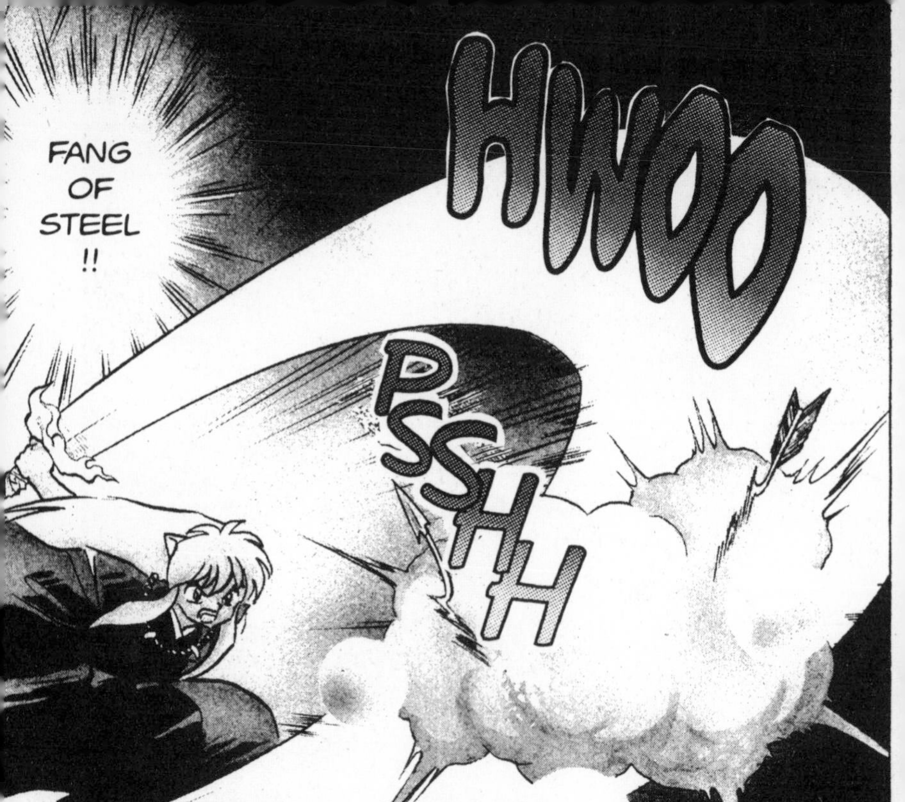

HWOO

FANG OF STEEL !!

PSSHH

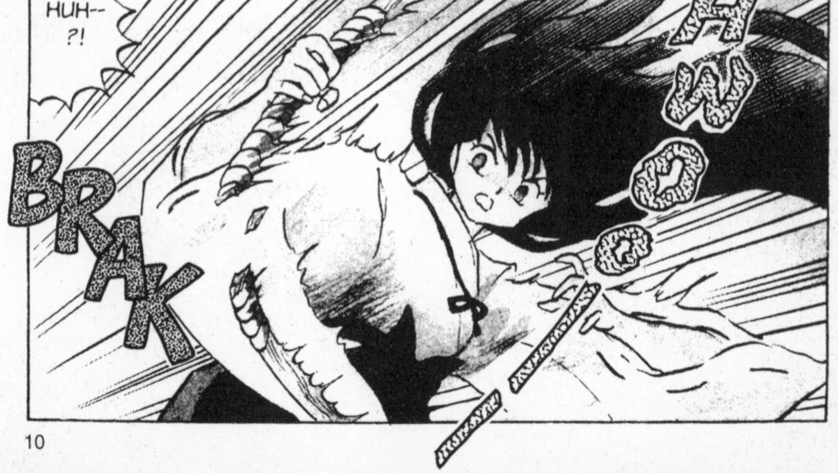

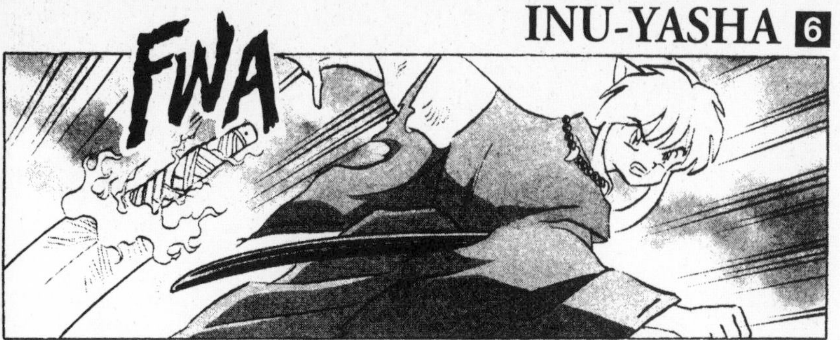
FWA

HE'S THROWING AWAY THE TETSUSAIGA... ?!

GPPP
NGH !

GRNN...
WHAT TRICKERY IS THIS, INU-YASHA...?

SHUT UP.
I'M NOT EVEN **DREAMING** ABOUT MAKING YOU CARE ABOUT ME, NOT ANY MORE...

BUT I WILL **NOT** JUST STAND HERE AND ALLOW MYSELF TO BE EXECUTED FOR SOMETHING I NEVER DID!
YOU... NEVER DID...?

DO YOU TAKE ME FOR A FOOL? THAT **WAS** YOU...

RIPPING THE SHIKON JEWEL FROM ME...
DECEIVING ME...TEARING ME OPEN WITH THOSE TALONS...

IF THE JEWEL FALLS INTO THE HANDS OF DEMONS, ITS DEMONIC POWERS MUST ONLY GROW. IT SHALL NEVER BE DESTROYED!
HOW-EVER...

DO YOU THINK I'M A HUMAN?
YOU ARE!
HALF HUMAN, AT LEAST.

IF IT IS USED TO MAKE YOU HUMAN...
THE JEWEL SHALL BE PURIFIED...AND SHALL MOST LIKELY VANISH INTO AIR.

KIKYO...
WHAT WILL HAPPEN TO YOU?
I AM SHE WHO GUARDS THE JEWEL... IF THERE IS NO JEWEL...

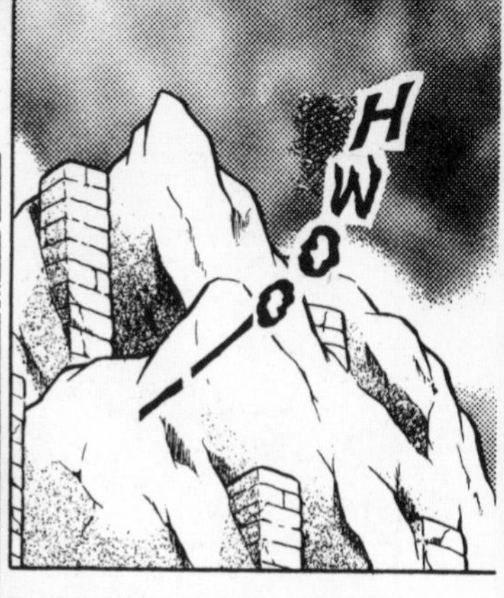
HWOO

I SHALL BECOME BUT A WOMAN.

YOU SAID YOU WOULD BECOME HUMAN.
THAT TIME...

WE WOULD LIVE OUR LIVES TOGETHER...
AND AS HUMANS...

DO NOT SAY IT!
I MEANT IT!

AND I DARED TO IMAGINE...THAT I MIGHT TRULY LIVE MY LIFE WITH YOU...
I WAS AN INNOCENT FOOL!

SHUT UP!!

GGG

YOU WENT THROUGH HELL LIKE ME.
KIKYO... I UNDER-STAND...
INU... YASHA...

...WAS TWICE HARD FOR YOU...

FWA
GET AWAY FROM HER!
N-NO, INU-YASHA...
RPOP
PAH
UGH!

SO LONG AS YOU ARE ALIVE, I CAN-NOT REST!
MY SOUL... CANNOT MOVE FROM THAT SPOT...
I DIED HATING YOU...
!
DESTROY THE BODY SHE'S IN!!
INU-YASHA--

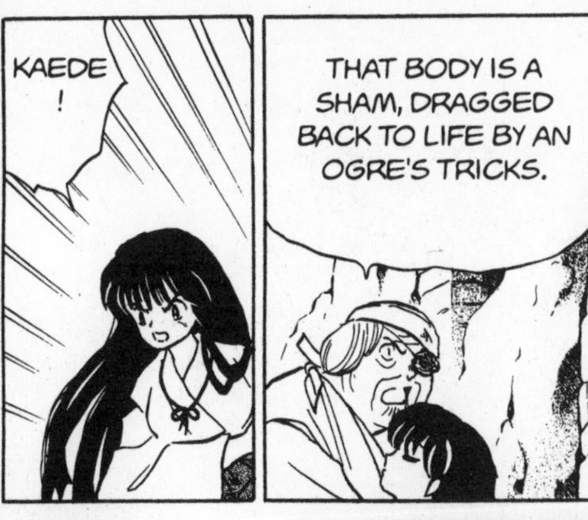

ALL THAT MATTERS, INU-YASHA...IS YOUR DEATH...!

HWO..

GUH...

GRNN...

KRAK

KAGOME... !

GWUHHH

P-P-POP

WHAT...
?!

HER
SOUL
IS...
!

GHOOOO...
NO...
NOT YET...
MY SOUL... IS BEING RIPPED FROM ME!!
NO !!

KAGOME... YOU...
YOU WERE NOT MERELY A SOULLESS HUSK?!
DOOOOM
DOMSH
SHHH

UNH...

...
KAGOME...
KIKYO...
ARE YOU FINALLY AT PEACE...?
!
WOBBLE...

SHE STILL MOVES.....?!
KIKYO!

UNGH...
OBBLE...

SCROLL TWO

A SOUL ASUNDER

WOBBB...
KIKYO... !
UNH...
YOBBLE...
DO YOU STILL HAVE SOME SOUL LEFT IN YOU?!
!
WHAT MOVES THIS BODY IS NO MORE THAN KIKYO'S HATRED...
URASUE !
HEE HEE...
HYUUUU...

MOST ALL OF THE SOUL SEEMS TO HAVE RETURNED TO THAT LASS'S BODY...

IT SEEMS IT SUITS HER WELL...
YET THE DARK POWER OF VENGEANCE STAYS BEHIND TO PLAY IN THE BONE AND GRAVESOIL PLAYGROUND I HAVE MADE...
H'OOO
H'OO

INU-YASHA...!
SHHH

PEH!

HOW... IRONIC...
NOW SUCH A VENGEFUL DEMONESS...
THE WOMAN WHO WAS ONCE SUCH A PURE THING...
RRRM
RRRM

HUFF.
HUFF.
ZPP

IF I REMAIN NEAR "HER"...
THE REST OF MY SOUL SHALL BE DRAWN BACK INTO HER AS WELL.

I MUST GET AWAY...

!
ZZZP
KRRRRRR

PAKK

KIKYO...

IT CAN NOT STAY THIS WAY...
KIKYO...

GO BACK INSIDE KAGOME.

TO DIE... ?
YOU DARE ASK ME...

UGH...

HWOOO——

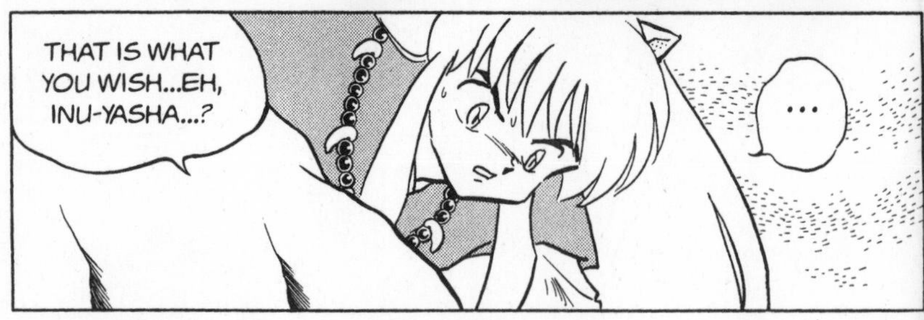

I... WILL... *NOT*... !

!

GYNN

WAAH !!

P-PAK

F-FOOL...
STOP IT...!
PSH PSH PSH PSH

THE DAY I DIE IS THE DAY YOU DIE!
I HAVE TOLD YOU ALREADY!
P-P-PAAAA

KLATTA
KRAK

GAH
DMP
DMP
DMP

!
KIKYO--!

WHY,
CURSE
IT...

WHY
MUST IT
END LIKE
THIS...?!
KLATTA

50 YEARS AGO...
A PRETENDER
IN KIKYO'S FORM
SHOT ME WITH
THAT ARROW...

THEN
BORROWED
MY FORM AND
ATTACKED
KIKYO...

SOMEONE...
HAD A GRUDGE
AGAINST US
BOTH...

INU-
YASHA...
SH...
BUT
WHO...
AND
FOR WHAT
FOUL
PURPOSE...
SHKK...

HOW'S KAGOME... ?

SHE HAS NOT AWAKENED, STILL.

...WHAT OF MY ELDER SISTER... ?

FALLING FROM SUCH A HEIGHT... THERE'S NO CHANCE...

I'M SORRY...

I COULDN'T SAVE HER...

I SEE...

THE PEACE OF DEATH IS BETTER THAN A LIFE IN A BODY OF BONE AND GRAVESOIL, WITH A SOUL OF NOUGHT BUT HATRED.

IT IS FOR THE BEST...

FOR THE BEST....

IT'S LIKE SHE'S BEING TORTURED BY NIGHT-MARES...
UHH...

.....
EH... ?!

I WONDER IF SHE'LL STILL BE THE SAME KAGOME...
WHEN SHE WAKES...

HERS WAS STILL A SOUL FORCED BACK FROM DEATH.
NO MATTER THAT IT RETURNED BACK INTO KAGOME'S BODY...

KAGOME... !
IF ANY OF MY SISTER'S CONSCIOUSNESS REMAINS... THERE MAY BE TROUBLE...
BLINK

KAGOME... !

OH !

HWAA

OH...

HUHH...

KAGOME...

HUHH...

HUHH...

...THAT'S ALL...?

OH. AND ENGLISH TOO.

...SHE'S STILL THE SAME KAGOME...

WHEW...

HUH...? WH-WHAT HAPPENED TO URASUE...?

AND KIKYO...

...

IT'S OVER, KAGOME.

WHAT...?

HYUUU...

REST IN
PEACE,
KIKYO...

SH...

ZZKK...
VWAA
BLIK

ZH...

GG...

INU-
YASHA...
ALIVE...
I'M
ALIVE...
!
ZHKK...

THEN...
YOU REALLY DON'T REMEMBER ANYTHING...?!
NOPE...
NOTHING...
I'M SORRY.
NO...
IT'S NOTHING TO APOLOGIZE ABOUT.

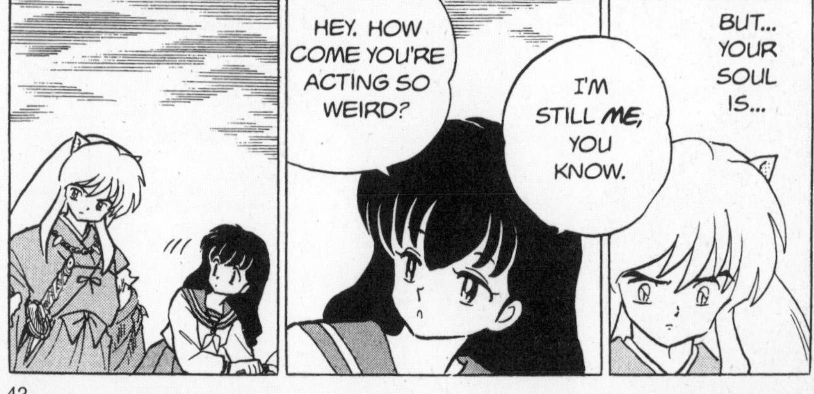

HA! YOU FINALLY LOOKED ME IN THE EYE!

GLINT

EH... ?

YOU'RE MORE YOURSELF WHEN YOU'RE ANGRY, YOU KNOW.
SHUT UP !

WHAT IS THIS... ?
WHEN I SAW KAGOME SMILE...I FELT RELIEVED...
...LOOKS LIKE HE'S CHEERING UP.
AYE...
KAGOME... SHE IS A WONDROUS CHILD...

EVEN THE POWERFUL SOUL OF MY SISTER...
COULD NOT SUBDUE HER.

THIS CHILD...
...IS NOT JUST ANY REINCAR-NATION.

SCROLL THREE

MONK ON THE MAKE

THIS TIME, IT **MUST** BE A PRIEST OF HIGH VIRTUE!
WELL...
HE DOES **CLAIM** TO BE SO, BUT...
ALL RIGHT. LET HIM ENTER. IF HE FAILS, CHASE HIM OUT LIKE ALL THE REST.
HOLY ONE...
PLEASE UNDERSTAND THAT IF THE DEMONS ARE NOT EXORCISE FROM HER HIGHNESS, TH HOUSE CANNO OFFER EVEN BOWL OF GRUEL...
I UNDER-STAND.

PRINCESS! A MONK IS HERE TO SEE YOU!

...

I HAVE GRASPED THE SITUATION.

MY LORD, REMOVE ALL YOUR HOUSE-HOLD FROM THE PREMISES... EXCEPT FOR THE PRINCESS.

UNDER-STAND THIS...

NOW...

IF YOU REMOVE YOURSELF OBEDIENTLY, I WILL FORGIVE YOU WITH A MERCIFUL HEART.

CHNK...

GNNG...

SHHH--

P-POP

SO! A WEASEL DEMON IN YOUR TRUE FORM, EH?!

HMM?! THAT SPARKLE...
Pff...
DGGG
IS IT A SHARD OF THE JEWEL ?!
EEEEEEEE...
WH-WHAT....? THE SHRIEK OF A BEAST... ?!
WHAT IS HAPPENING IN THERE...?

MASTER, WOULD YOU HAVE US LOOK.....?
NO... WAIT...
HE SAID NOT TO PEEK, FOR ANY REASON...
AND BESIDES, WHO NEEDS TO GET SPLATTERED BY EXORCISTIC BACKWASH?
B- BUT MASTER...
IT MORE LIKE THE SOUNDS OF RANSACKING THAN...
KLATTA
G-DUMP
JUST WAIT! JUST WAIT!

CAW CAW
SO HE SAID THIS TINY WEASEL TRANSFORMED ITSELF INTO LORD AMIDA...
AND WAS DEVOURING YOUR SOUL...?
BUT WHAT ABOUT THE MONK...?
WITHOUT EVEN GIVING HIS NAME, HE DEPARTED.
BLUSH
TM TM TM
M-M-MASTER!

EVERYTHING OF VALUE HAS BEEN STOLEN!!
EVEN THE HORSES!!
KRII
NOW... WHERE CAN I SELL THESE...?

I AGREE.
KAGOME, I SWEAR THERE'S SOMETHING WEIRD ABOUT INU-YASHA...
CHIRRRING
KLATATATA
PAM
HEY, WAKE UP! ANYONE HOME!?
THAT'S WHAT I MEAN BY WEIRD!
MWONG
WILL YOU BE QUIET? I'M TRYING TO THINK HERE.

WHEN THE JEWEL'S PUT BACK TOGETHER I CAN BECOME A FULL DEMON...

...BUT THEN WHAT?

I DON'T KNOW ANY MORE...

IF I BECOME A FULL DEMON,

WILL MY HEART GET STRONGER TOO?

SO THAT I CAN FORGET ABOUT KIKYO...

...AND NEVER AGAIN BE LED ASTRAY BY ANY WOMAN...?

HSSH
CURSE THE MAN...

IS THIS SHIKON JEWEL SHARD...
MY ONLY PROFIT...
JUST MY LUCK...

AFTER ALL THE TROUBLE I WENT THROUGH TO BRING THE GOODS!
AN ANTIQUE DEALER TAKING ADVANTAGE OF A MAN OF THE CLOTH....
SHKK SHKK

HM ?
WHEE!! A HOT SPRING!! I'M SO HAPPY!!
PLSH

PEOPLE... THIS FAR UP IN THE MOUNTAINS... ?
WHAT'S THIS... ?

MMM... FEELS SO GOOD--!

SHHooo

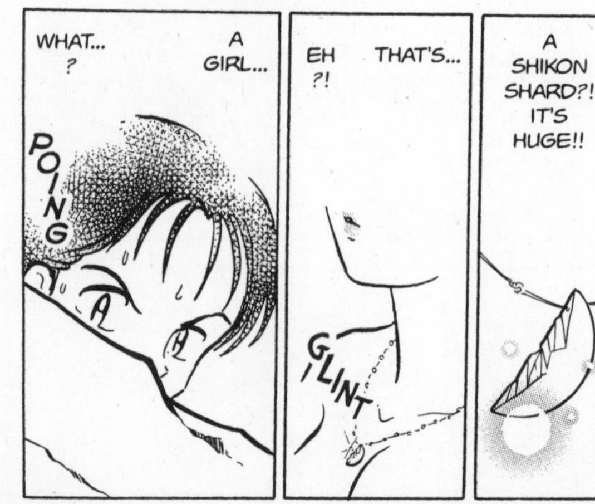

DON'T WORRY.
I'M *NOT* TEMPTED.
OH, THANKS-- !

GEEZ....
HE'S EVEN RUDE WHEN HE'S POLITE!

O' COURSE I GUESS...
I'M NO WARRIOR-BABE LIKE KIKYO.
NOT THAT I KNOW MUCH ABOUT HER...

HUH ?
SHIPPŌ, WHY ARE YOU TAKING OFF *YOUR* CLOTHES ?
VWIP VWIP VWIP
I'M GONNA HOP IN TOO!

NO YOU DON'T.
WHY DON'T YOU COME IN?
GRNG

WHAT ?!
I'VE BEEN WONDERING ABOUT IT FOR A WHILE...

YOU KNOW WHAT THEY SAY, THE MORE THE MERRIER!
WHY DON'T YOU EVER SLIP IN WITH KAGOME, EH?
BACK WHEN PA AND MA WERE ALIVE, I ALWAYS TOOK BATHS WITH THEM!
HEY!
SO HOW FAR HAVE YOU ACTUALLY GONE WITH KAGOME?
LISTEN. YOU'RE TOO YOUNG TO UNDERSTAND THIS, BUT...
PSST
AND JUST WHY WOULD I TELL A THING LIKE THAT TO *YOU*?!
RRNG RRNG RRNG
WHA...?
...SO PERFECT...
IT'S SO QUIET...

SSSS...

♪

MNSH...
I'M OKAY! GET OUTTA HERE!
SHOO, SHOO!
KIII
IT'S A MONKEY!
BRBBL

WITH SOME FELLOWS, IS SHE....?
WHAT A PITY.

I DO SO HATE TO GET ROUGH, AFTER ALL...
OH WELL...
KRAK

BWOK
OW-WOO!

MASTER MIROKU-- PLEASE FORGIVE ME--!
TONK TONK
KEEP IT UP... I'M PAYING YOU, REMEMBER...

MAN...HOW LONG ARE YOU GONNA SULK...?
YOU GOT TO SEE ME NAKED TOO, SO WE'RE EVEN, RIGHT ?

LEAVE ME OUT OF THIS...
HE DID SEE, DIDN'T HE?
I SAW NOTHING !

AND DURING THE CONFUSION... I'LL TAKE THE GIRL...

YUP.
SO I SHOULD ATTACK THE MALES, YES?

SHF

IF I USE ***THIS...***

THEY'LL ALL DIE!

SCROLL FOUR

JEWEL THIEF

MASTER MIROKU, IF SOMETHING SHOULD GO WRONG, YOU WILL RESCUE ME...WON'T YOU?

I TOLD YOU NOT TO WORRY.

SHF

pip

TRANS-FORM!

BWA

DIE !!
DMDMDMDMDMDM
WHA-- ?!
K-SHHAMM
YEEE !

GG..
GG..
GG..
UNH!
WAAH!

I- INU-YASHA--!
KALANG...

HK
!

EEK!
DNSH

...
KTATATA

WH- WHO **ARE** YOU--?!
PLEASE. DO NOT FEAR.

I AM ONE WHO SERVES BUDDHA. I WILL DO NO CREATURE HARM.
GRINN

WHAT AM I, A PRIZE IN A CEREAL BOX?!
WHEN I ATTEMPTED TO RETRIEVE THE SHIKON SHARD, I DID NOT REALIZE THAT YOU CAME WITH IT.
KATATA

NNNG...?!
!

KAGOME ?!
KATATA

OUT OF MY WAY, BEAST !
DONK
WH-WHO IN THE SEVEN HELLS IS THAT...?!

SHHHH
IF YOU DON'T GET OUT OF MY WAY... !
GWOO
EEP !

I'D DO BETTER ALONE....
SHKK
FEH.
HWOOO
HUH ?!
PSSHH
DNNG
AARGH !

BASH
AS YOU WISH!
LET ME GO!
INU-YASHA!
KALANG...
ZZZZ
DAMMIT! LOOK AT WHAT HE DID TO ME!
WHAT IN THE WORLD DID HE DO?
THAT MOMENT... HIS RIGHT HAND...
HE SAID HE WAS A SERVANT OF BUDDHA, BUT...
WHO AND ***WHAT*** WAS ***THAT*** BASTARD?!

I SUDDENLY FELT LIKE I WAS BEING PULLED TOWARDS HIM BY SOME INCREDIBLE WIND...
BUT HOW COULD HE DO THAT... AND FROM SUCH A DISTANCE...?!
...

HHH

SHOOT!
WHAT?

THAT "SERVANT OF BUDDHA" STOLE MY *BIKE*!
....

YOU WERE ALMOST KIDNAPPED YOURSELF!
IS THAT ALL THAT BOTHERS YOU?!

BAH.
I TAKE MY EYE OFF OF YOU FOR ONE SECOND, CURSE YOU, AND...

......
......
INU-YASHA...

MM ?
I'M SORRY.

D-DON'T BE. I-IT'S NOT THAT I WAS WORRIED ABOUT YOU OR ANYTHING, YOU KNOW. I WAS JUST...

JUST CONCERNED OVER THAT JEWEL SHARD YOU'RE...

THAT'S WHAT I MEAN.

IT LOOKS LIKE HE STOLE
...THE SHIKON SHARD, TOO.

KRIK

BWOOM

HE WON'T GET AWAY WITH IT!

YAMA YAMA
STAY A WHILE AND PLAY WITH US--!
WHEEEEE---
OH, HE'S A BEAUTIFUL ONE!
I AM SUCH A FOOL!
SIGH...
O-HO HO HO HO HO
THESE ARE YOUR FINEST...?
AS YOU WISHED, I HAVE GATHERED MY FINEST GIRLS.
TMM TMM TMM

HEY, INU-YASHA. YOU DONE YET?

QUIET!

THERE ARE SO MANY DIFFERENT SCENTS HERE... IT'S NOT GOING QUICKLY...

CAW
CAW

HEY...
MAYBE HE'S NOT HERE ?
HE **MUST** BE-- !
SNIF SNIF

BUT WHY WOULD A THIEF DILLY-DALLY AROUND A PLACE LIKE THIS...?

SNIF SNIF
OH !!

EH ?
AIEE-- DEMONS-- !!
DM DM DM

HEY, YOU !
GWRRR
BICYCLE THIEF!

Y-YOU'RE THE--

HEH...
KR-KRAK
"FROM HELL TO HEAVEN," THE GREAT BUDDHA WRITES. MY SPIRITS SOAR!
This is truly a paradise !
Is it this-- ?
SLAP SLAP
GYNN

UNGH... !
RECKLESS...
RECKLESS...
SH-SHH
Yaa!
Aiee!

VNN
NOW. LET'S SETTLE THIS!!
WHOOPS.

BAH...

THIS IS NOT SOMETHING A DEMON SHOULD POSSESS.

THEN I'LL GIVE IT A POINT--YOUR DEATH!

SHHH

KKAK

HE PARRIED THE TETSUSAIGA ?!
THIS...IS NO ORDINARY MONK!
AND IF THE POINT BE ***YOUR*** DEATH...?

SCROLL FIVE
WIND TO NOWHERE

HYOOO
WHO IN THE SEVEN HELLS ARE YOU?!
WHAT IS IT--?!

MY NAME IS MIROKU
I USE MY SPIRITUAL GIFTS TO HELP THE NEEDY.
'TIS THE LORD MONK, ABOUT TO EXORCISE A DEMON!
YAMA YAMA
SAVE IT FOR THE FOOLS, THIEF!
A MONK WHO HELPS THE NEEDY?!

YOU WOUND ME.
LEAVE THE SHARD OF THE SHIKON JEWEL IN MY CARE,
INU-YASHA...

PRIK...
HE... KNOWS MY NAME...

I'LL MAKE IT SO YOUR GLIB LITTLE MOUTH NEVER TELLS ANOTHER LIE AGAIN!!
HEH...
WHOOO
DM-DM-DM-DM-DM-DM

WAKAKA

MY...

YOU'RE A STRONG ONE!

HE'S BLOCKING MY STROKES...

SO EASILY...!

WHOK

HA!

RETURN THE SHARD YOU'RE HIDING IN YOUR SLEEVE!

UNLESS YOU'D RATHER DIE!

...

HEY--

TRYING TO ESCAPE AGAIN, ARE YOU?!

VSSHH

GOOD PEOPLE, PLEASE REMOVE YOURSELVES AS FAR FROM HERE AS POSSIBLE...

OR YOUR ***LIVES*** WILL BE IN DANGER!

OH?

HIS... HIS HAND!!

PRAISE BUDDHA!
KLATTA

HWOO
!

TAOT TAOT TAOT
SNORT
ZZHHHHH

WHAT--?!
THAT WIND--
PULLING US IN--?!
GAR

ROOAR

WHI-HINNY..

UNNH!

RRRRORRR
HOW LONG CAN YOU HOLD OUT, MM?

KI-RRRIII--
PAKPAK
IT WILL DEVOUR US ALL--!
FLEE--!

THIS ISN'T YOUR EVERYDAY BUDDHIST MONK!
IT'S LIKE A BLACK HOLE...

NKH...!

DOOOOO

DOOOO...

GIVE UP!

ONCE PULLED IN, YOU'LL NEVER COME OUT!

SHUT UP!!
I'LL SLICE THAT TUNNEL OFF YOU-- ARM AND ALL!
!
IT'S NO USE...
YOU'LL BE SUCKED IN, BLADE AND ALL...
EH?!

FWOOO

WHAT--?

KAGOME?!

GUHH!

WHNNN
DMG
ZZZZZZZZZ
KAGOME!
WHY...?!

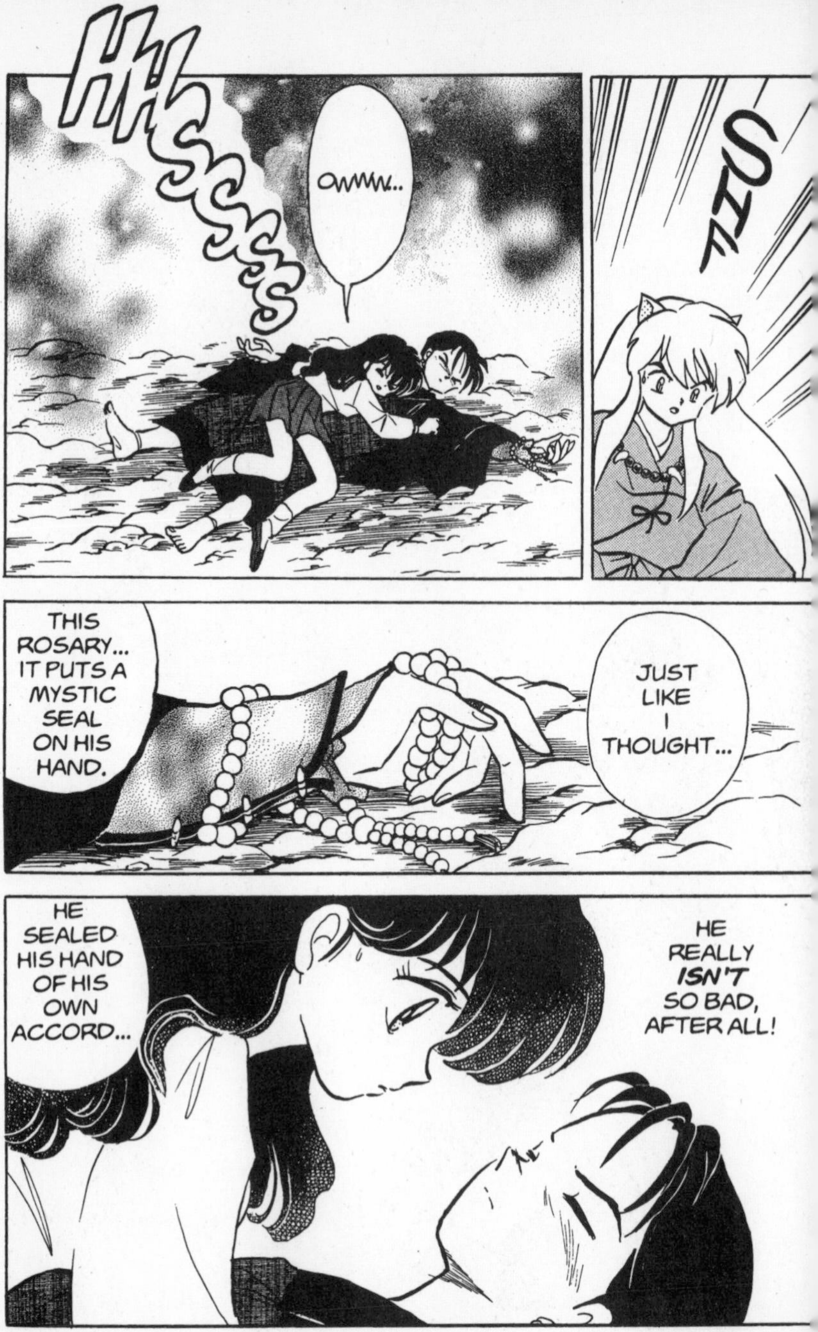

SHF

HISSSS

OWWW...

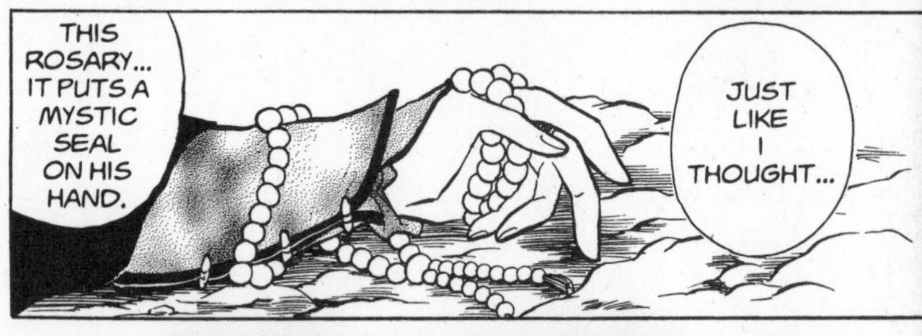

SCROLL SIX
THE CURSED HAND

...YOU LEAPT INTO THIS ON PURPOSE?!
KAGOME YOU...
LISTEN TO ME...
IF MIROKU HAD USED THE POWER IN HIS HAND...
...HE COULD HAVE KILLED US A LOT EARLIER!

I'M SURE WE CAN WORK THINGS OUT IF WE TALK...

FWA
KNING
MWUH

FLINCH
RRUB RRUB

PWIK...

WHAT KIND OF MONK ARE YOU?!
BRRR...
ON SECOND THOUGHT... KILL HIM!
HFF- HFF-

I CAN EXPLAIN.
PLEASE. CALM YOURSELVES.

I AM GATHERING SHARDS OF THIS JEWEL OF FOUR SOULS...
...ONLY IN ORDER TO FIND AND DESTROY A CERTAIN DEMON...
...A DEMON CALLED NARAKU.
"ABYSS"...?
THIS BOTTOMLESS CHASM IN MY HAND,
...WAS CUT BY NARAKU'S CURSE.

YOU DON'T KNOW?!

NARAKU PIERCED MY GRANDFATHER'S HAND-- STRAIGHT THROUGH HIS SEALING SCROLL--

AND ESCAPED HIM FOREVER.

THE HELLHOLE I HAVE OPENED IN YOUR HAND
SHALL ULTIMATELY SWALLOW YOU...

AND YOUR CHILDREN... AND YOUR CHILDREN'S CHILDREN.
SO LONG AS I AM ALIVE, THIS CURSE SHALL BE PASSED DOWN UNTIL YOUR LINE HAS VANISHED FROM THE EARTH.

...

THIS TUNNEL WIDENS EVERY YEAR, AND THE WINDS... WELL, THEY DO GET STRONGER.

IF I CANNOT DEFEAT NARAKU...
...THEN, IN A FEW YEARS,
I TOO SHALL BE DEVOURED.

YOU MEAN... YOU'RE GOING TO DIE?
YES.

THAT IN ITSELF FRIGHTENS ME LITTLE...
IT IS A FATE TO WHICH I HAVE LONG BEEN RESIGNED...

BUT...
TO DIE LEAVING NARAKU LOOSE IN THE WORLD...
ESPECIALLY SINCE THE SHIKON JEWEL THAT WAS THOUGHT TO HAVE BEEN DESTROYED FIFTY YEARS AGO HAS NOW REAPPEARED, ITS PIECES SCATTERED EVERYWHERE.
NARAKU WILL SURELY TRY TO GATHER THE SHARDS TO OBTAIN EVEN GREATER DEMONIC POWER.
YOU SEE...

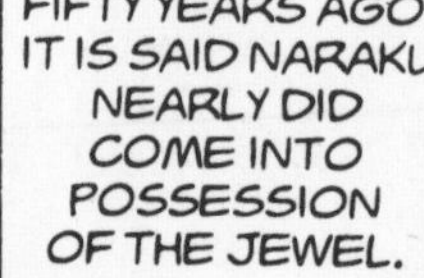
FIFTY YEARS AGO, IT IS SAID NARAKU NEARLY DID COME INTO POSSESSION OF THE JEWEL.
IT SLEW THE PRIESTESS WHO WAS GUARDING IT, AND...

!

THE BASTARD WHO TOOK MY FORM AND KILLED KIKYO... FIFTY YEARS AGO...
IT KILLED A PRIESTESS?!
YOU SAID...
SHAHH
...IT HAD TO BE NARAKU!

DON'T YOU THINK IF I KNEW...

...I'D HAVE HUNTED IT DOWN AND DESTROYED IT LONG AGO?

SNARING ME AND KIKYO WITH ITS LIES...

FANNING HATRED AND DISTRUST BETWEEN US...

...AND IT'S STILL ALIVE... STILL HUNTING THE SHIKON JEWEL?!

I'LL
FIND IT...
I'LL
KILL IT...
...FOR
YOU,
KIKYO!

...

IF WE KEEP GATHERING THESE SHARDS...

...WE'RE BOUND TO RUN INTO NARAKU, RIGHT?
OH! HOW... WHEN...?

SO LET'S DO IT TOGETHER.

HM?

INU-YASHA HAS NO INTENTION OF HANDING IT OVER, RIGHT?
NOT WHILE I LIVE!

SO, YOU SEE?
...

YES, BUT... WELL...

...I'VE NEVER BEEN GOOD AT WORKING WITH OTHERS...

BUT IF YOU DON'T DEFEAT NARAKU SOON, YOU'LL DIE, RIGHT?

LADY KAGOME...
...YOU ARE CONCERNED FOR MY WELFARE?

WELL.. YEAH...
THEN I HAVE A FAVOR TO ASK OF YOU.
GYNN

PLEASE BEAR MY CHILD.

TWIK

I THOUGHT YOU WERE ONLY HER TRAVELING COMPANION
OH. FORGIVE ME.
INU-YASHA...
IF I SEE YOU LAYING ONE HAND ON KAGOME...!
I CAN'T GET ANYTHING RIGHT, CAN I?
...BUT OF COURSE, IF YOU LOVE HER...
WHAT?!
OH-HO...
THAT'S RIGHT! INU-YASHA'S INTERESTED IN SOMEONE *ELSE!*
SHE'S JUST A SHARD DETECTOR, THAT'S ALL!
LISTEN, FOOL--!
OH!
...AND *THEY'RE* GOING TO WORK TOGETHER?
ONE MUST BE MORE CONSIDERATE TOWARD THE LADYFOLK.
CAN'T I TRUST YOU WITH ANYTHING?!
YOU COULD LEARN SOME THINGS FROM MIROKU.

BRACE UP, DEAR COMRADES!
WE HAVE ALMOST REACHED MY STRONGHOLD!
KLOP KLOP

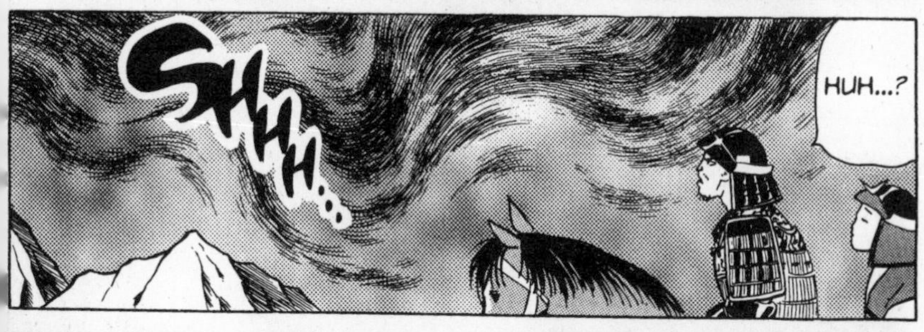
SHHH...
HUH...?

SHKA SHHKA
?!

TROPHIES FOR THE MASTER!
HUNT THEM DOWN!

DEMONS--!!
W-WAAH--!

BRUTAL WARFARE...
SHHF...
EEEEEEE...!

THIS WASN'T WAR.
THE LIVER HAS BEEN TORN FROM EVERY ONE OF THEM.

REST IN PEACE.
I'D SAY.
DEMONS...?

THIS IS NOT THE WORK OF MINOR DEMONS...
I SUSPECT THEY POSSESS A SHIKON SHARD.

THE SMELLS...
NOT JUST BLOOD...
...INK
YES! THE SMELL OF CHARCOAL INK.

MIROKU!
LET ME TELL YOU THIS NOW...

I HAVE NO INTENTION OF BEING YOUR "COMRADE"...
AND I'M ***NOT*** HANDING OVER THE SHARDS.

SO... "THE EARLY BIRD GETS THE WORM," EH...?

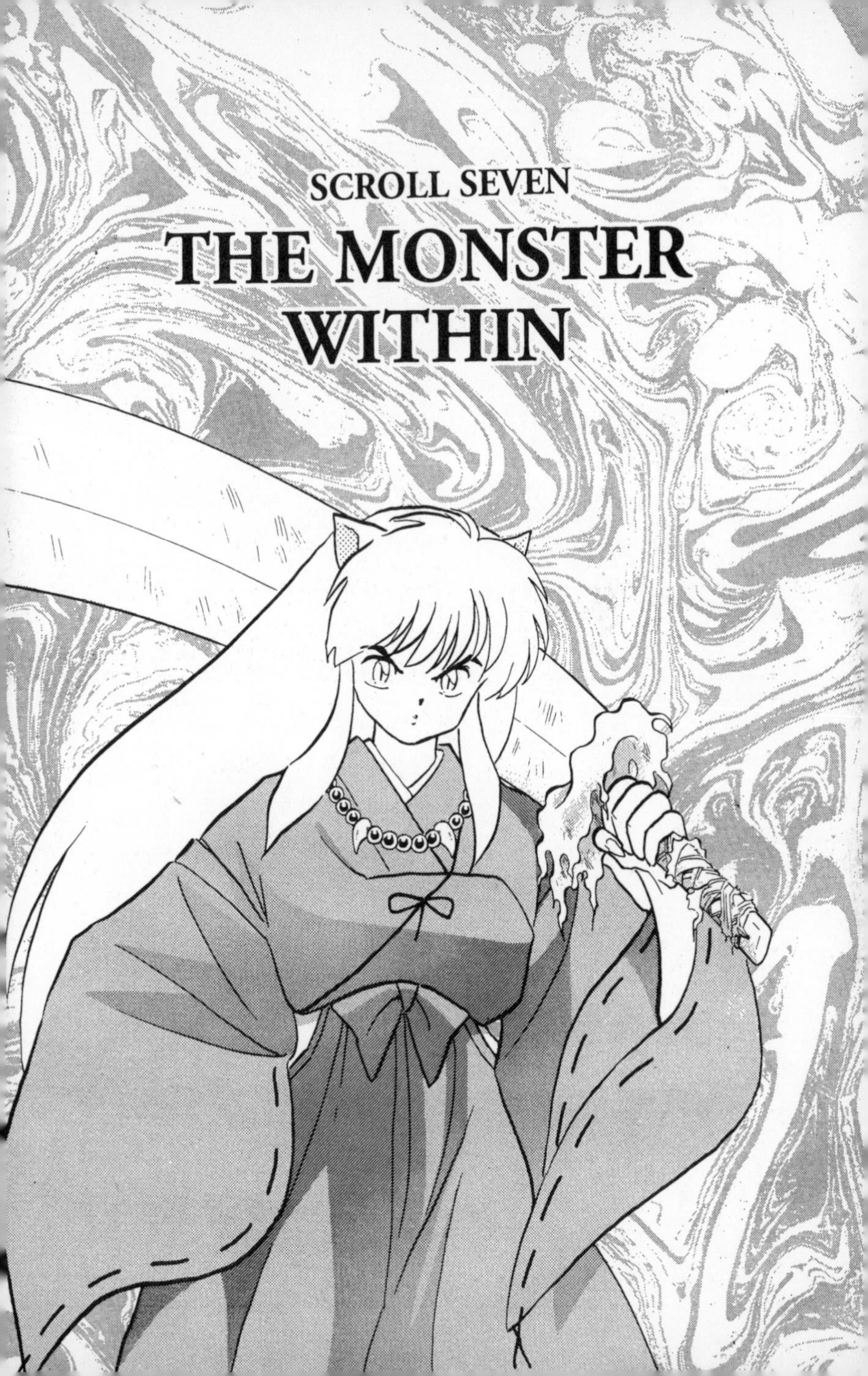
SCROLL SEVEN
THE MONSTER
WITHIN

WE SHALL PART HERE.
HENCEFORTH... I MUST FORGE ON ALONE.

SIGH.
CHRIRIN
SHTOMM
YEAH. THAT MIROKU SEEMED SO... DEPENDABLE...
IDIOT! WE COULD FIND ALL THE SHIKON SHARDS SO MUCH FASTER IF HE'D JUST WORK **WITH** US!
EH?!!
TWIKTWIK

I SMELL... ***INK!***
AIEE--! P-PLEASE, SOMEONE, HELP--!
HUH--?! SO ***THIS...*** IS THE SOURCE OF THE SMELL?
SNUF SNUF SNUF
AAAAH-- MY ERRAND SCROLL--!
INU-YASHA-- ***SIT!***
WHAT-ARE-YOU-***DOING?!***
GYUUU
HE'S JUST A NORMAL PERSON!
I'M SO SORRY--!
WH-- WH-- WH--!
B-BMP B-BMP

THE SCENT OF INK LINGERED ON THE AIR!
IN THE WAKE OF THE DEMONS...

I TOLD YOU!
GEEZ... WHAT ARE YOU SO WORKED UP ABOUT?

UH...
WHY DO YOU HATE HIM SO MUCH?
IF WE DON'T ACT QUICKLY, THAT BASTARD MIROKU WILL STEAL ALL THE SHARDS!

WHAT...?!

I'M KIDDING, OKAY...?
I'M KIDDING.

I LOVE 'EM!
AND YOU LIKE DROOLING LECHERS LIKE HIM?!

HELLO! WILL YOU LISTEN TO ME PLEASE?!
THROB THROB THROB
IS THAT... IS THAT WHAT SHE REALLY WANTS...!?

NOT A CLUE TO A SINGLE SHARD...
WHAT IS THIS WORLD COMING TO?
YAWWW--
VILE, BELLY-CRAWLING WORM!
DONK

BE THOU NOT CRUEL IN OUR NAME...

DESIST.

IT IS BEST THAT YOUR HIGHNESS PROCEED.
PTUU
...

SHE IS BEAUTIFUL... BUT...
IF I LEAVE HER BE, SHE WILL NOT LIVE LONG.
HER SHADOW IS FAINT.

I-IS OUR HIGHNESS *WELL*...?
KEH KEH

...
WOBBLE...

SAVING THE LADY IS MY MOST URGENT TASK...
I THINK...

AS IF MY ART COULD "DEFILE" NOBILITY...!
TRUDGE

...THEY KNOW NOTHING!
FOOLS... CATTLE...

KSSH...

SOON SHE WILL BE MINE... AND MINE ALONE...
AAH... THE PRINCESS BY DAY IS STILL AS BEAUTIFUL.

EEP!
GWII

HEY.
HOW ABOUT LENDING ME A ***HAND?***
WHAT--?!

BWAAH
L-LET GO OF ME!
YOU WON'T SLIP AWAY FROM ME!
GNNG
!

HUH?!
BAM
HO!
BOOM
AN OGRE...?!

DOM

GRII...

YOU... STOP THERE...!

WHAT'S GOING ON?!

THAT MAN IS A DEMON?!

NO... NO...

ZHHH...

HE'S MORTAL...

HAH!

SHYUN
YES--!

HE DID IT...!
THE BIGGER THEY ARE, THE...
HEH!
BLACK BLOOD?!
OH!
DOSSHH
DOSSHH
EH?!
PEH... PEH...PEH...
P-TOOOO...!

NOT ONLY BLOOD...
DRRRIP...
BUT LIVER... AND INK...!

HIS DOG-NOSE IS TOO SENSITIVE... THE STENCH DID HIM IN.
ZHF
HEY...

WH-WHAT'S WRONG?

KWRR KWRR
HUH?!

EVERY NIGHT YOUR HIGHNESS SUFFERS TERRIBLE DREAMS...?
SO...

DEMONS... THEY COME...
DREAMS OF WHAT?

...FERRYING TO AN ESTATE UNKNOWN THIS NOBLE PERSONAGE...
...WHERE WE IN A CHAMBER ARE LEFT ALONE.

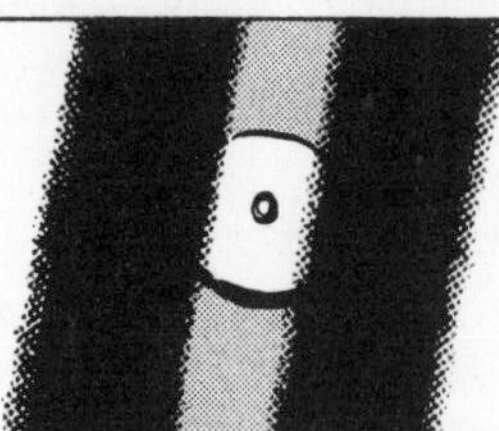
AND YET... WE FEEL SOMETHING...
FROM SOMEWHERE, SOMEONE PIERCES US WITH A GAZE...

WITH EACH PASSING NIGHT THE PRINCESS WASTES FURTHER AWAY.
LORD MONK, IS MY DAUGHTER BY A DEMON POSSESSED?

THERE CAN BE NO DOUBT. IT MUST BE EXORCISED IMMEDIATELY...

MY LORD, MIGHT YOU GRANT ME SOME TIME ALONE WITH THE PRINCESS?

BE AT EASE, YOUR HIGHNESS.
I SWEAR TO YOU BY THE BUDDHA THAT I WILL SAVE YOU.
BUT... UM...
YES?

I KNOW IT'S A BIT MUCH TO ASK AS COMPEN-SATION...
BUT WILL YOUR HIGHNESS BEAR MY CHILD?
GYUU
HSSS
EH?

JUST LIKE I THOUGHT!
YOU SAY THAT TO ALL THE GIRLS!
EH?
WELL, WELL-- MIROKU!
KRIII
WEREN'T YOU LOOKING FOR SHIKON SHARDS?
AWP! LADY KAGOME!

AND THIS WAS THE BUFFOON YOU WANTED TO *JOIN* US, KAGOME?!!
WELL.. *YOU* WERE UN-CONSCIOUS...

THIS IS THE LAST PLACE I'D HAVE EXPECTED YOU TO FIND ME...
AND THESE CREATURES ARE...?

SHAA

HOW...
HOW DID HE KNOW THAT I'VE BEEN COLLECTING HUMAN LIVERS...?

NO MATTER!
I HAVE NOTHING TO FEAR...

...FOR BEHIND ME...
...STANDS AN ARMY OF THOUSANDS OF *OGRES!*

SCROLL EIGHT
THE MASTER PAINTER

HWOOO--

BRRRR
BRRRR

LIKE THIS... SHE LOOKS LIKE AN **OGRESS!**
WHY...?

NO--!!
KSSHH

...A STRANGE ARTIST, YOU SAY?

HE WAS MORTAL... NOT A DEMON HIMSELF...

PRIN-CESS...
I SHALL SEND AN ESCORT FOR YOU ONCE AGAIN TONIGHT.

BUT HE WAS MANIP-ULATING AN OGRE.
SO I'M THINKING...

YOU THINK HE MAY BE DRAWING ON THE POWER OF A SHIKON SHARD...
OF COURSE..
WHAT IS THE MATTER, INU-YASHA?
OH, COME ON. HOW LONG ARE YOU GONNA SULK?
FEH.
WHAT IS IT, INU-YASHA? THIS DISCUSSION BENEATH YOU?
NOTHING!
WHAT--?!
JEALOUS--?!
YOU-- YOU--
YOU CAN'T BE THAT JEALOUS!
WHAT'S WRONG WITH ASKING LORD MIROKU FOR A LITTLE HELP?

LADY KAGOME...
YOU MUST HAVE SEARCHED SO DESPERATELY FOR ME...
STARE
BOP
BOP
BOP

HUH? NO, NO.
WE JUST HAPPENED TO BE PASSING THIS PLACE AND DETECTED A SHIKON AURA, THAT'S ALL.

EH?
PFF...

WHAT?!

GYUU--

YOU HAVE TWO... NO, THREE OF THEM, DON'T YOU?

WHAT... SHARP EYES YOU HAVE...

DOMP
DOMP

SIT!
DOMF

WHY DIDN'T YOU TELL ME, WENCH...?!

THESE ARE ONES THAT I GATHERED MYSELF. IF YOU TAKE THEM, YOU'RE THIEVES.

YOU CALL US THIEVES?!

UH-- LORD MONK...?

YES?

WHAT SPOKE YOU ABOUT SAVING THE PRINCESS...

...YOU HAVE NOT FORGOT

AH.

OF COURSE NOT, YOUR LORDSHIP.

SHE IS MY HIGHEST PRIORITY!

WE HAVE A BAD FEELING ABOUT THIS.....

IF EVERY NIGHT, SERVANT-DEMONS APPEAR...

AND CARRY YOUR HIGHNESS TO AN UNKNOWN ESTATE THEN...

...EH?
GSSH
INU-YASHA... YOU'VE COME TO ASSIST ME WITH THIS MISSION AS WELL?
HAH.
THAT'S NOT WHY I'M HERE!
IT'S JUST...
IT'S COMING NEAR...!
FWOO...
THAT SMELL AGAIN!

KARA KARA KARA KARA...

THE SMELL OF THAT PAINTER!!

BLOOD AND LIVER AND INK...

DSSH

I'M SURE OF IT NOW--

THAT PAINTER'S INVOLVED IN THIS TOO SOMEHOW!

GWO..

PRIN-CESS...
WHERE ARE YOU...?
SHF SHF

KARA...
KARA KARA
AH!

SHHH
PEEK
P-PRIN-CESS...

NOW, PRINCESS...

OUR LORD MASTER IS AWAITING.

KARAA
DOLOOP
WHERE'S THE PRINCESS...?!
AWP!

FWOO...

I WILL NOT ALLOW...

ANY TO STAND IN MY WAY...!

MRMR MRMR

THE AURA OF DEMONS!

GRMGRMGRM...
HERE IT COMES!

!
PAINTINGS...?!
PAINTINGS!
WH-WHAT IS THIS...?!

IF YOU'RE SCARED, MIROKU-- FEEL FREE TO GO HOME!

NO! THIS IS *MY* MISSION!

ZHAA

SCROLL NINE

THE ARTIST'S DREAM

I AM FOND OF PAINTING SCENES OF HELL.

IN MY QUEST TO DEPICT EVER MORE TERRIBLE SCENES...
I BEGAN TO TRAIL BEHIND BATTLES AND SKETCH THE CORPSES CONTORTED BY PAIN.

IT WAS ONE SUCH DAY, IN A POOL OF BLOOD...
THAT I DISCOVERED THAT MOST INTRIGUING SHARD.

ITS BEAUTY WAS BEAUTIFUL.
GLEAMING LIKE A RAINBOW THROUGH SPILT BLOOD AND BITS OF LIVER.

I TOOK THE SHARD HOME.
BLOOD AND LIVER AND ALL...

I DIS-SOLVED IT IN THE INK, AND PAINTED AN OGRE.
BLUP...

THEN, BY A MIRACLE, MY OGRE CAME TO LIFE.
MORE...
MORE BLOOD... MORE LIVER...

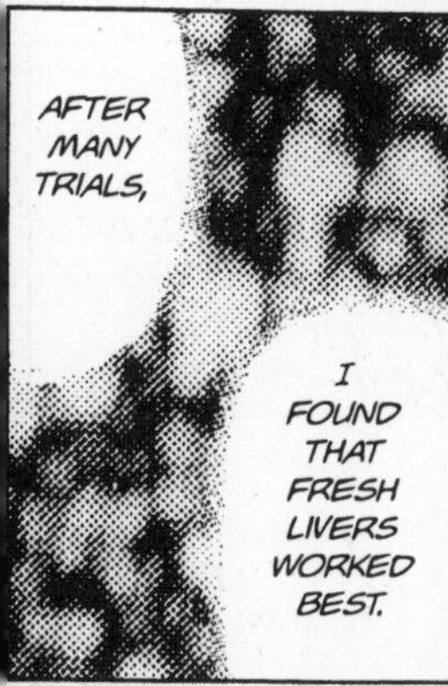
AFTER MANY TRIALS,
I FOUND THAT FRESH LIVERS WORKED BEST.

AT FIRST, I MERELY USED MY ASSISTANTS.
LATER, I WAS FORCED TO AMBUSH PASSERSBY.

BUT I KILLED A LITTLE TOO OFTEN...
AND I COULD STAY IN THE CITY NO LONGER.

AND THEN, IN THIS LAND TO WHICH I HAD FLED...

I ENCOUNTERED THE PRINCESS.

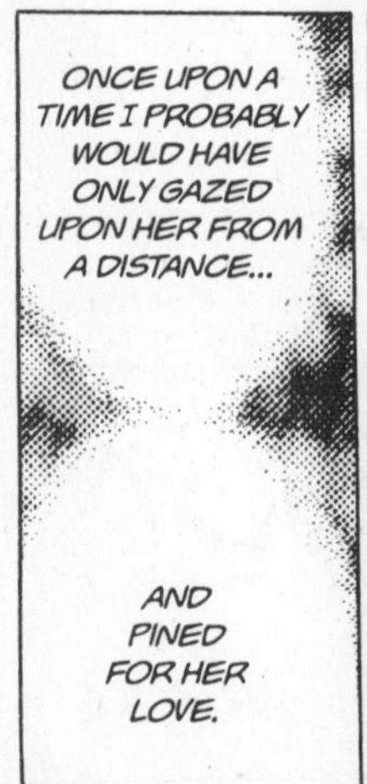

HYOOOO
OUT OF MY WAY-- ALL OF YOU!
WHSSH
WHSSH

EEEK!!
DOMP

THERE'S NO END IN SIGHT!
THEY KEEP COMING!
HA!
I'LL PUT AN END TO 'EM!

DM DM DM DM DM DM

INU-YASHA...?

ZHH
!

THE STENCH OF THE OGRES' BLOOD!
TOO MUCH FOR HIM!

WHAT HAP...
WHAT...
FUMP

KRAK
BLACH

...
L-LORD MIROKU...

STAND BEHIND ME, BOTH OF YOU!

I MUST UNLEASH THE *ABYSS*!

HSH

HWOOOOSH
WHAT...?

MY... GOD... !

SSSHHH

NNH... !

IT... TAKES SOME-THING OUT OF ONE...
THIS IS...THE FIRST TIME I'VE SUCKED IN SO MUCH DEMONIC POWER...

LORD MIROKU !
SHMPooo

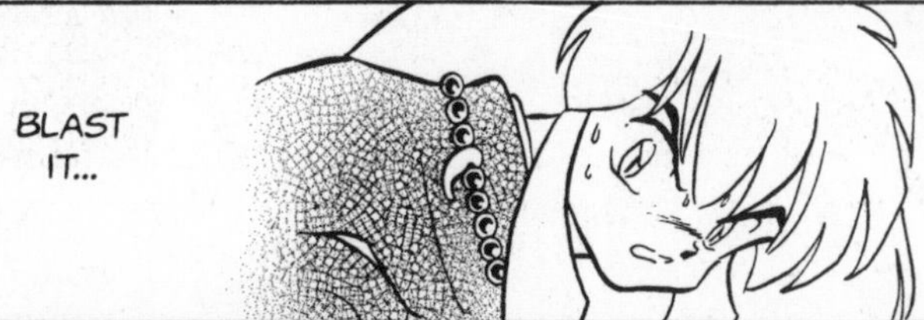
WHY'D I HAVE TO BE SAVED BY *HIM*...?
BLAST IT...

RRRMMMMBBLL
KRIIK KRIIK

NOW WHAT ?!

KRRIKRAK

WOOOSSHH

I'M TAKING IT BACK FROM HIM!
WHERE'S THE SHIKON SHARD, KAGOME?

GLINT...
...

NOT FOR LONG.
DM
IN THAT BAMBOO TUBE!

RRR
ZMP

SEE THIS, MONK ?!
THOUGHT I'D LET *YOU* DO ALL THE SHOWING OFF?!

HE...*UH*... SAYS THINGS STRANGELY.
ALLOW ME TO TRANSLATE.

"THANKS, LORD MIROKU!
I'LL TAKE IT FROM... *UH*...
...HERE..."
HE SAYS THINGS STRANGELY, INDEED.

HOOOOOO
NKH...
CLNCH...

FWW

ZHHHH

HE NEVER RUNS OUT.
IF HE CUTS THEM DOWN, HE'LL BE KNOCKED OUT BY THE SMELL AGAIN!

OUT OF MY WAY !!

I'VE GOT NO USE FOR THE LIKES OF YOU!!
WOK
WH-WHAT KIND OF SORCERY IS THAT?!
I THINK IT'S CALLED "SLUG-GING."

WHAT'S WRONG?
ALL OUT OF OGRES?
HOOOOOO

SCROLL TEN
TAINTED INK

LET'S END THIS...

HOOOOOOOOO

HE HAS CORNERED HIM.

BUT...

INU-YASHA CAN'T USE HIS BLADE!

IF HE CUTS THAT SNAKE, THE STENCH WILL KNOCK HIM OUT!

FOOL!

I PAINTED THE MONSTER YOU RIDE!

HSH

!

HWOOOOFFFF...

!
INU-
YASHA
!
HOOF
NOT EVEN YOUR
BONES WILL BE
LEFT BY THE FIRES
OF HELL!
GGG

NNH...
GG...
HOOSSHHHHH
THE SHARD...
RRR...
GIVE IT UP...
NO...

DO YOU THINK I'LL LET MYSELF BE BEATEN BY A HUMAN?!
I AM DEMON!
SHHH
AH... WAIT.
PLEASE! SPARE MY LIFE!

I-I WAS JUST LIKE ANYONE...
IF I HAD NEVER STUMBLED UPON THIS...
SHUDDER
...
FEH.
CHING...
HE WON'T KILL HIM...?!

HENH
ZZHH
VOP
!
ARH!
GGGG
WOK WOK WOK WOK
OH...

WOK
LET GO !!

HOOSSHHHH

SHA

DMM

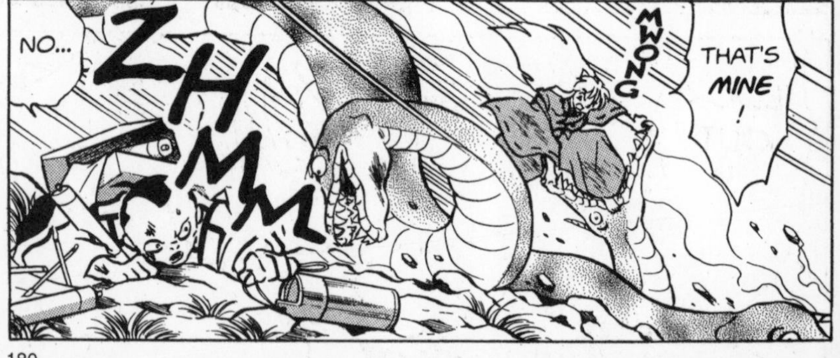
THAT'S MINE !
MWONG
ZHMM
NO...

VMM
THERE'S NOWHERE TO GO!
SHLUMP...
SHMP SHMP
HUHH *HUHH* *HUHH*
BLUP...
!
LET GO...
LOOK OUT!

UH...
ZNG
DMMP

HELP... ME...
SSHHHHHH...
UGH... !
GNNG
GLUSH...
I TOLD YOU...
IDIOT.
SHHHHH...!

!
BLUP BLUP BLUP
THE... THE INK...
B-BUT WHY... HOW...?
BLOOD...
THIS INK WAS MADE WITH BLOOD AND LIVER...
IT CAME TO TAKE THE BLOOD THAT THE ARTIST SPILLED.
FF
M...?
THIS...
HE WAS TRYING TO PAINT THE PRINCESS.

IT IS TOO DANGEROUS FOR ME TO TOUCH.
ULP.
PWIP
HMP.
THE JEWEL SHARD THAT WE SUFFERED SO MUCH TO OBTAIN IS SOILED BY DEMONIC POWER, TOO.
KIIIN
HOW CAN ONE PAINT SUCH PURITY... WITH SUCH TAINTED INK?
WHAT A FOOL.
THIS SHARD...
WHO SHOULD HOLD IT?
ping..
WHAT... ?

THERE'S NO DISCUSSION HERE!
BUT LORD MIROKU HELPED US OUT.
PLEASE, LADY KAGOME... YOU HOLD IT.

UH...
YOU SURE?
THAT WAS NO TRICK OF MY EYES JUST NOW...

THIS MAIDEN...
SHE PURIFIED THE SHARD OF DEMONIC POWER...

HEY, DID ANYBODY EVEN *THINK* OF ASKING *ME* TO CARRY THE STUPID THING?!
WE MIGHT HAVE, SHIPPŌ...
IF YOU HADN'T BEEN HIDING!

FOOL.
WHAT ARE YOU PRAYING OVER *HIM* FOR?

FOR THE DEAD, THERE IS NEITHER GOOD NOR EVIL.
ALL THAT REMAINS IS THE MERCY OF BUDDHA.

ERCY !
I SWEAR I'LL NEVER UNDERSTAND YOU HUMANS!
INU-YASHA.

YOU COULD HAVE SLAIN HIM HAD YOU WANTED TO.
BUT YOU DID NOT.

THAT IS MERCY.

HA!
DON'T MAKE ME LAUGH!

TO BE CONTINUED...

About Rumiko Takahashi

Born in 1957 in Niigata, Japan, Rumiko Takahashi attended women's college in Tokyo, where she began studying comics with Kazuo Koike, author of *Crying Freeman*. She later became an assistant to horror-manga artist Kazuo Umezu (*Orochi*). In 1978, she won a prize in Shogakukan's annual "New Comic Artist Contest," and in that same year her boy-meets-alien comedy series *Urusei Yatsura* began appearing in the weekly manga magazine *Shônen Sunday*. This phenomenally successful series ran for nine years and sold over 22 million copies. Takahashi's later *Ranma 1/2* series enjoyed even greater popularity.

Takahashi is considered by many to be one of the world's most popular manga artists. With the publication of Volume 34 of her *Ranma 1/2* series in Japan, Takahashi's total sales passed *one hundred million* copies of her compiled works.

Takahashi's serial titles include *Urusei Yatsura, Ranma 1/2, One-Pound Gospel, Maison Ikkoku* and *InuYasha.* Additionally, Takahashi has drawn many short stories which have been published in America under the title "Rumic Theater," and several installments of a saga known as her "Mermaid" series. Most of Takahashi's major stories have also been animated, and are widely available in translation worldwide. *InuYasha* is her most recent serial story, first published in *Shônen Sunday* in 1996.

COMPLETE OUR SURVEY AND LET US KNOW WHAT YOU THINK!

☐ Please do NOT send me information about VIZ products, news and events, special offers, or other information.

☐ Please do NOT send me information from VIZ's trusted business partners.

Name: ______________________________

Address: ______________________________

City: ____________________ **State:** ________ **Zip:** ____________

E-mail: ______________________________

☐ **Male** ☐ **Female** **Date of Birth** (mm/dd/yyyy): ____/____/________ (Under 13? Parental consent required)

What race/ethnicity do you consider yourself? (please check one)

☐ Asian/Pacific Islander ☐ Black/African American ☐ Hispanic/Latino

☐ Native American/Alaskan Native ☐ White/Caucasian ☐ Other: ____________

What VIZ product did you purchase? (check all that apply and indicate title purchased)

☐ DVD/VHS ______________________________

☐ Graphic Novel ______________________________

☐ Magazines ______________________________

☐ Merchandise ______________________________

Reason for purchase: (check all that apply)

☐ Special offer ☐ Favorite title ☐ Gift

☐ Recommendation ☐ Other ______________________________

Where did you make your purchase? (please check one)

☐ Comic store ☐ Bookstore ☐ Mass/Grocery Store

☐ Newsstand ☐ Video/Video Game Store ☐ Other: ____________

☐ Online (site: ______________________________)

What other VIZ properties have you purchased/own? ______________________________

____

How many anime and/or manga titles have you purchased in the last year? How many were VIZ titles? (please check one from each column)

ANIME	MANGA	VIZ
☐ None	☐ None	☐ None
☐ 1-4	☐ 1-4	☐ 1-4
☐ 5-10	☐ 5-10	☐ 5-10
☐ 11+	☐ 11+	☐ 11+

I find the pricing of VIZ products to be: (please check one)

☐ Cheap ☐ Reasonable ☐ Expensive

What genre of manga and anime would you like to see from VIZ? (please check two)

☐ Adventure ☐ Comic Strip ☐ Science Fiction ☐ Fighting

☐ Horror ☐ Romance ☐ Fantasy ☐ Sports

What do you think of VIZ's new look?

☐ Love It ☐ It's OK ☐ Hate It ☐ Didn't Notice ☐ No Opinion

Which do you prefer? (please check one)

☐ Reading right-to-left

☐ Reading left-to-right

Which do you prefer? (please check one)

☐ Sound effects in English

☐ Sound effects in Japanese with English captions

☐ Sound effects in Japanese only with a glossary at the back

THANK YOU! Please send the completed form to:

NJW Research
42 Catharine St.
Poughkeepsie, NY 12601

All information provided will be used for internal purposes only. We promise not to sell or otherwise divulge your information.